Contents

What shall we have for dinner
Meat
Poultry
Cooked and canned meats and poultry
Fish
Eggs
Cheese and milk
Dry beans and peas
Bread and other cereal foods
Lunch-box main dishes

Money-Saving Main Dishes

By

Richard D. Hines

What shall we have for dinner ...

This is easy to answer after you have decided on the main dish.

The main dish is especially important in meal planning. It is the hub around which the rest of the meal is built, and often it carries a large proportion of the cost of the meal. Usually the main dish is the main source of protein—so essential to building and repairing body tissues.

In this booklet are recipes and suggestions for about 150 main dishes—easy to make, hearty, and economical. Most of the dishes give four liberal servings; a few provide more.

Most of these main dishes furnish about a fourth of the day's needs for protein. For those that provide less, additional protein foods are specified in the menu suggestion following the recipe. Or you may prefer to increase the amount of protein rich food in the main dish—by adding more meat, for instance, to a main-dish soup, salad, or casserole. The rest of the day's protein will come from milk used as a beverage, and from cereals, bread, and other foods eaten as part of the day's meals.

You get top-rating proteins (as well as other important nutrients) in foods from animal sources, as in meat, poultry, fish, eggs, milk, cheese. Some of these protein foods are needed each day; and it is an advantage to include some in each meal.

Next best for proteins are soybeans and nuts and dry beans and peas. When these or grain products are featured in main dishes, try to combine them with a little top-rating protein food, if you can.

No one food is exactly like any other food and no food is complete in all nutrients. Milk products are high in calcium; meats are low. Meat, poultry, eggs, and beans are good sources of iron; milk is low in it. One kind of B vitamin abounds in meats, another in milk, and a third in whole grains. The best way to be sure of a good diet is to use a variety of main dishes and wide choices of other foods to complete the meal.

Main-dish Proteins From a Variety of Sources

To supply a fourth of the day's protein requirement, a main dish for a family of four must contain about 2 ounces of protein. Although this averages ½ ounce (15 grams) per person, it will not necessarily be divided equally among the family members—men and teen-age boys and girls will need somewhat more; women and younger children, somewhat less. There follows a list of foods commonly used in main dishes, together with the quantity needed to provide the ½ ounce of protein.

Approximate Amounts of Some Foods That Provide About ½ Ounce (15 grams) Protein

	As purchased
Meat:	
Cuts with only small amounts of bone or visible fat (as beef stew meat, veal cutlet, rolled rib roast, round steak, boned rump roast, tongue)	3 ounces
Cuts with moderate amount of bone and visible fat (as standing rib roast, rump roast with bone, lamb shoulder roast, pork chops)	4 ounces
Cuts with much fat or bone (such as bacon, pork sausage, spareribs)	5 ounces or more
Luncheon-meat mixtures (as bologna, frankfurters)	3½ ounces
Chicken (as roasters, stewing hens):	
Whole, dressed (with head, feet, bone, viscera weighed in)	4 to 5 ounces
Ready-to-cook (head, feet, viscera removed)	3 to 4 ounces

Canned or boneless, lean	2 ounces
Turkey:	
Whole, dressed (with head, feet, bone, viscera weighed in)	4 ounces
Ready-to-cook (head, feet, viscera removed)	3½ ounces
Fish, canned or boneless (as salmon, tuna)	2½ ounces
Eggs, in shell	4½ ounces (2 large or 2½ medium-size)
Milk:	
Fresh, whole or skim, or buttermilk	14½ ounces (1¾ cups)
Evaporated	7 ounces (⅞ cup)
Dry, nonfat	1½ ounces (5½ tablespoons)
Cheese:	
Cheddar	2 ounces (½ cup, grated)
Cottage	2½ ounces (5 tablespoons)
Peanut butter	2 ounces (4 tablespoons)
Dry beans, except soybeans (as lima, navy, kidney)	2½ ounces (about ⅓ cup)
Soybeans, dry	1½ ounces (about 3 tablespoons)

A Daily Food Guide

As you plan your main dishes, do your overall menu planning too, keeping in mind the different kinds of foods that are needed for an adequate diet. Plan to serve foods from each of these four groups every day:

• Milk group—milk in all forms (fluid whole or skim, evaporated, dry, buttermilk). For children, the equivalent of 3 or more cups of fluid milk daily; for teenagers, 4 or more cups; for adults, 2 or more cups.

• Meat group—meat, poultry, fish, eggs; as alternates, dry beans, peas, and lentils; nuts, peanuts, peanut butter. Two or more servings daily.

• Vegetable-fruit group—vegetables and fruits of all kinds. Four or more servings, including a citrus fruit or other fruit or vegetable important for vitamin C daily and a dark-green or deep-yellow vegetable for vitamin A at least every other day.

• Bread-cereal group—all breads and cereals that are whole grain, enriched, or restored. Four or more servings daily.

Other foods—the fats and oils, sugars, and unenriched cereal products used in cooking or added to foods at the table—will help to round out meals and satisfy appetites.

Looking at our national diet, we find that nearly half of our protein comes from the meat group. But about a fifth comes from bread and other cereal foods. And the milk group provides about a fourth.

We can then rely on these three food groups to provide the protein of our main dishes. We need not have protein-deficient diets even if we economize on meat. For we can get protein from other foods, using them as suggested in the money-saving recipes given in this booklet.

Meals to Suit the Family

Foods to serve with the main dishes are suggested at the end of each recipe. Choices will depend on available supplies, cost, the season, and what the family likes. If the protein in the main dish is limited, care should be taken to include in the meal the other protein-rich foods suggested in the menu (such as salads or desserts containing egg or milk) or dishes equally high in protein, to raise the total protein for the meal.

In some homes, noon is the time for the big meal of the day. In others, only at night can the family gather around the dinner table. In still others, where everyone is physically active, a big meal is needed both noon and night, and perhaps also at breakfast. But whenever the meal, the hearty dishes described in this booklet will help you to use a variety of economical foods to supply the protein your family needs.

If you cannot use the recipe exactly as stated, perhaps one of the suggested variations will be suited to the foods you have at hand, your family preferences, or the facilities you have for cooking.

Meat ...

Meat is too valuable, for its flavor and its protein, iron, and B vitamins, to waste any of it. Part of the cook's skill is to make good use of every bit.

Cook meat bones with beans or soup to extract all possible flavor, and nutrients too.

Use rendered fats in gravies and sauces and ground cracklings in quick breads.

The following information on the yield from various cuts of meat will help you decide how much to buy to get enough lean meat for a main-dish serving. It will also help you figure the cost per serving.

Much bone or gristle—a pound yields 1 to 2 servings. Examples are shank, brisket, plate, short ribs, spareribs, breast of lamb or veal.

Medium amount of bone—a pound yields 2 to 3 servings. Examples are whole or end cuts of beef round, veal leg or shoulder, ham with bone in; also steaks, chops, or roasts from the loin, rump, rib sections, or chuck.

Little bone—a pound yields 3 to 4 servings. Examples are center cuts of beef round, or ham; also lamb or veal cutlets.

No bone—a pound yields 4 to 5 servings. Examples are ground meat, boneless stew meats, liver or other variety or boneless meats.

Buying Meat

Homemakers who are after good buys at the meat counter will consider the grade and the cut.

Federal grades of beef usually found on the market are Prime, Choice, Good, Standard, and Commercial. Markets vary in the grades of beef carried and may offer only one or two, as for example, U. S. Choice and U. S. Good. The lower grades cost less per pound than similar cuts of higher grades and usually contain more lean. Beef is the meat most often sold with a U. S. Grade stamp, but lamb, mutton, veal, and calf are sometimes federally graded. Pork usually is not graded.

The cut refers to the part of the animal from which the meat comes. The buyer can usually save money by using the less tender cuts of beef and the less popular cuts of pork, lamb, and veal. These cuts cost less per pound but provide the same valuable protein as the more expensive cuts. Variety meats, such as liver, heart, and kidney, also provide high return in nutrition for money spent.

In comparing costs, consideration must be given to the amount of bone, fat, and gristle because they affect the cost of the lean edible portion.

It pays to buy the cuts best suited to the cooking methods you use. Do you know what to choose for pot roasts, stews, and soups? Here is a handy guide.

For pot roasts, Swiss steaks, smothered steaks, other braised meats.— Beef round, rump, sirloin tip, flank, chuck, short ribs, heart, and liver. Spareribs and ham hocks. Pork liver and heart. Thick pork chops or ham slices or shoulder steaks. Lamb shoulder, neck, breast, shanks, heart, and liver. Veal round, rump, shoulder, and heart.

For stews, soups, or to cook before creaming or frying.—Beef, lamb, or veal neck. Beef plate and brisket (fresh or corned). Tongue (fresh or smoked). Veal or lamb shanks, kidneys, brains. Pork kidneys and brains. Veal, lamb, or beef sweetbreads.

To Make Meat Tender

Good cooking can help make any cut of meat a favorite main dish with the family. Here are some of the methods that skillful cooks use for less tender cuts:

Long, slow cooking, as for braised meats and stews.—For extra flavor first brown meat in a little fat. To braise, use little or no liquid except the juices that cook from the meat. Cook, closely covered, with low heat. To stew, add water to partially cover meat, cover kettle, and simmer.

Chopping, pounding, scoring.—The foodchopper helps make meat tender. After chopping, any meat cooks as quickly as a tender cut. Pounding, or scoring with a knife, before cooking is similar in effect to chopping but tenderizes meat less.

Seasonings

Meat itself is usually flavoring enough for the main dish. It is often browned in a little fat to develop its flavor. In combination dishes, highly flavored or cured meats such as ham, dried beef, corned beef, and sausage may lend more flavor than fresh meat.

When the meat is limited, other foods will add zest and additional food values. Tomatoes, onions, parsley, chives, green peppers, celery, sour cream, lemon, nippy or smoked cheese—all contribute in both ways.

Other seasonings your family may enjoy with meat are bay leaf, catsup, chili, curry, garlic, marjoram, paprika, sage, soy sauce, sweet basil, tabasco sauce, thyme, worcestershire sauce. Since these are used in small quantities, they are not expensive in the long run.

Seasoning is especially important for meat-extending dishes. Meat loaves and other dishes which combine meat with bland foods such as macaroni, rice, or potatoes depend on skillful seasoning for their goodness.

A "boiled" dinner

    2 pounds spareribs
    1½ cups hot water
    4 medium-sized potatoes, pared and halved
    1½ cups canned or cooked green snap beans and liquid
    Salt and pepper

Brown spareribs in fry pan without added fat. Add water and simmer about 1 hour.

Add potatoes to meat and cook until tender—about 25 minutes.

Add beans and liquid the last 10 minutes of cooking. If raw beans are used, add with potatoes.

Season with salt and pepper. Skim off excess fat before serving.

Menu Suggestion

Serve with crisp lettuce, tomato, and celery salad, and apple betty with lemon sauce for dessert.

For Variety

Beef short ribs may be used with longer cooking.

Corned beef, meaty ham hock, or ham bone may be used in place of the spareribs. Cover with water and simmer about 3 hours or until tender. Omit salt, and continue as above. Good with sauerkraut.

A variety of vegetables may be used in a "boiled" dinner. In addition to potatoes, use onions, large pieces of carrot, and wedges of cabbage. Add cabbage about 20 minutes before serving, as it cooks more quickly than the other vegetables.

Scotch meat patties

¾ pound ground beef
⅓ cup milk
¾ cup quick-cooking oats
Salt and pepper
2 tablespoons cooking fat or oil
1 cup water
¼ cup chopped celery
¼ cup chopped green pepper
¼ cup chopped onion
1 teaspoon worcestershire sauce
1 tablespoon flour

Combine meat, milk, oats, 1 teaspoon salt, and pepper. Make very thin patties; brown on both sides in the fat or oil in a fry pan.

Add water and vegetables; season with worcestershire sauce, salt, and pepper. Cook covered over low heat 30 minutes.

Blend flour with a little cold water, add slowly to the mixture, and cook until thickened, stirring occasionally.

Menu Suggestion

Serve with candied sweetpotatoes, cabbage and carrot salad, with fruit and cookies for dessert.

For Variety

Meat Balls and Tomato Sauce.—Form the meat mixture into small balls and brown in fat. Remove from pan and brown the vegetables in the fat. Add ½ cup water and ½ cup tomato paste. Add meat balls and seasonings and cook covered over low heat. Thickening may not be needed. Serve over spaghetti.

Kidney stew

¾ pound veal or lamb kidneys
1½ cups diced potato
1 small onion, sliced
¾ teaspoon salt
1 tablespoon flour
1 egg yolk
Chopped parsley
1 tablespoon lemon juice

Cut the kidneys in half and wash well. Remove skin, blood vessels, connective tissue, and fat.

Cover kidneys with cold water, heat slowly to boiling, discard the water, and repeat the process until there is no strong odor and no scum on the water. Add about 1 quart fresh water and simmer kidneys until tender. Remove kidneys from broth and cut into small pieces.

Cook potato and onion in the broth. Add kidneys and salt.

Blend a little water with the flour, stir into broth. Cook a few minutes to thicken.

Stir some of the stew into the beaten egg yolk. Mix all together and add parsley and lemon juice. The heat of the stew will cook the eggs sufficiently.

Menu Suggestion

Serve with a green or yellow vegetable, apple and raisin salad, cookies or cake for dessert.

For Variety

Beef kidney may be used in place of veal or lamb if desired.

Soy meat loaf

¾ pound chopped meat
1½ cups vegetable liquid, tomato juice, or milk
2 ounces salt pork, diced (about ⅓ cup)
2 tablespoons chopped onion
½ cup chopped celery
¾ cup soy grits
2 tablespoons chopped parsley
2 teaspoons salt
¾ cup breadcrumbs
⅛ teaspoon pepper

Select one kind of meat or a mixture of two or more kinds.

Blend vegetable liquid, tomato juice, or milk with the meat.

Fry salt pork until crisp and remove from fat. Cook onion and celery in the fat for a few minutes.

Add all the ingredients to the meat and mix well.

Shape the mixture into a loaf and place on heavy brown paper on a rack in an uncovered pan.

Bake loaf at 350° F. (moderate oven) until well done and brown—about 1 hour.

Menu Suggestion

Serve with baked potatoes or squash, peas, and green salad, with apple crisp or peach cobbler for dessert.

For Variety

To vary the flavor, serve the loaf with brown gravy or tomato sauce.

Sweet-sour spareribs, Chinese style

    2 pounds spareribs
    1½ cups water
    ¼ cup raisins
    ½ teaspoon salt
    2 green peppers, cut in 6 pieces each
    1½ tablespoons cornstarch
    ¼ cup sugar
    ¼ cup vinegar
    Soy sauce

Cut spareribs into serving portions and brown in a fry pan over moderate heat—about 5 minutes on each side.

Add ½ cup of the water, the raisins, and salt.

Cover pan tightly and cook over very low heat 20 minutes.

Add green peppers. Stir in cornstarch blended with sugar, vinegar, and 1 cup of water.

Cover and continue cooking over low heat for 30 minutes. Stir occasionally and add more water as needed to prevent drying. Before serving add soy sauce to taste.

Menu Suggestion

Serve with rice or hominy grits and a green salad. For dessert, have fresh or baked fruit.

Spareribs in Another Way

Baked Spareribs.—Bake spareribs at 350° F. (moderate oven) until the meat is tender—about 1½ hours. Baste several times with a barbecue sauce, if desired.

Pork shoulder with savory stuffing

Remove the bones and any skin from a 5- to 6-pound fresh pork shoulder.

Sprinkle meat on inside with salt and pepper, and pile in some of the stuffing. Begin to sew edges of shoulder together to form a pocket, and gradually work in the rest of the stuffing. Do not pack tightly.

Sprinkle outside of shoulder with salt and pepper, and if desired with flour also.

Place the roast, fat side up, on a rack in a shallow uncovered pan. Roast without water at 350° F. (moderate oven) until tender—about 4 hours for a 5-pound shoulder. Turn roast occasionally. Remove strings before serving.

Serve with sweetpotatoes, fried apples, celery salad, and raisin pie.

Savory Stuffing

¼ cup diced celery and leaves
1 tablespoon diced onion
1 tablespoon chopped parsley
2 tablespoons cooking fat or oil
2 cups soft breadcrumbs
¼ teaspoon savory seasoning
Salt and pepper

Cook celery, onion, and parsley in fat or oil for a few minutes.

Add breadcrumbs and seasonings and stir until well mixed. This stuffing may be used with other meats and with poultry. Sausage, chopped tart apples, or chopped nut meats may be added.

Swiss steak

1 pound beef or veal rump or round, cut about 1 inch thick

Salt and pepper
Flour
Cooking fat or oil
2 cups cooked or canned tomatoes or tomato juice

Season meat with salt and pepper, sprinkle with flour. Pounding helps make the meat tender.

Cut meat into serving pieces and brown in a little fat or oil.

Add tomatoes or juice, cover, and simmer gently until meat is tender—about 1½ hours.

Menu Suggestion

Serve with mashed potatoes, corn, lettuce salad, and prune whip.

For Variety

Swiss Steak With Brown Gravy.—Use water instead of tomatoes. When done, remove meat, add water if needed to make 1 cup total liquid, and if necessary thicken with flour blended with cold water.

Swiss Steak, Onion Gravy.—Add 2 cups sliced onions to Swiss Steak With Brown Gravy during the last half hour of cooking.

Spanish Steak.—Follow recipe for Swiss Steak, using ¾ pound meat. Brown ½ cup chopped onion and 1 chopped green pepper in fat. Cook 1 cup macaroni in boiling salted water. Mix macaroni, onions, and pepper with the tomato sauce and serve over meat.

Sausage with sweetpotato and apple

½ pound sausage
2 medium-sized sweetpotatoes

3 medium-sized apples
½ teaspoon salt
1 tablespoon flour
2 tablespoons sugar
½ cup cold water
1 tablespoon sausage drippings

Cut link sausage into ½-inch pieces.

Fry until well done. If bulk sausage is used, shape it into small balls before frying or break it up as it cooks.

Pare and slice potatoes and apples.

Mix salt, flour, and sugar together and blend with cold water.

Arrange layers of potatoes, apples, and sausage in a baking dish, pouring flour-sugar mixture over each layer. Top with apples and sausage, and add drippings.

Cover; bake at 375° F. (moderate oven) until apples and potatoes are tender —about 45 minutes.

Menu Suggestion

Serve with a crisp green salad. For dessert have a well-chilled creamy rice pudding made with eggs and milk to supplement the protein from the small serving of meat. If you double the amount of sausage in the main dish, you will not need to choose a dessert that supplies additional protein.

For Variety

Replace the sausage with thin slices of smoked pork shoulder, or thin shoulder pork chops, well browned.

Main-dish soup

3 or 4 pounds meaty soupbones (beef or veal shank or shortribs)
Drippings or other fat
Bay leaf, if desired
3 cups diced vegetables
Salt and pepper

Have bones cracked and remove small slivers. Brown in fat in a large kettle. Cover with water, add bay leaf, and simmer until meat is tender enough to fall from bones—3 to 4 hours.

Add vegetables such as onion, carrots, and potatoes during the last half hour of cooking.

Remove bones from broth. Cut up meat and add to the soup. Season to taste.

Menu Suggestion

Serve with green salad and fruit pie. If there isn't much meat, serve cottage cheese salad or serve cheese with pie.

For Variety

Onion Soup.—Omit other vegetables. Slice 4 medium-sized onions and brown in drippings before adding to the meat broth. Serve piping hot, topped with toasted bread sprinkled with grated cheese—the traditional French way of serving.

Beet Soup.—To 1 quart broth and meat add 2 large beets, grated or ground, 1 cup chopped cabbage, and 2 chopped onions. Simmer until vegetables are tender. Season with salt and pepper. Top each serving with sour cream.

Brown beef stew

1 pound boneless stewing beef

Salt and pepper
Flour
Drippings or other fat
1½ cups water
3 potatoes, diced
2 onions, sliced
3 carrots, diced
1 cup raw snap beans

Cut meat into inch cubes. Sprinkle with salt and pepper, roll in flour, and brown in the fat.

Add water, cover, and simmer until almost tender—2 to 3 hours.

Add vegetables, season with salt and pepper, and continue to simmer, covered, until vegetables are done. Stir occasionally.

Menu Suggestion

Serve with coleslaw or green salad, and a baked pear or peach for dessert.

For Variety

Green-Tomato Stew.—Use ½ chopped onion in place of sliced ones. Brown with the meat. Use 2 medium-sized green tomatoes, quartered, instead of beans.

Lamb or Veal Stew.—Use breast or neck of lamb or veal in place of beef and ½ cup diced turnips instead of beans.

Quick Stew With Hamburger.—Use hamburger in place of stewing meat. Brown the meat, add vegetables and water and simmer. The stew will be done in half an hour or less.

Meat-potatoburgers

¾ pound chopped raw beef
¾ cup chopped or coarsely grated raw potato
¼ cup chopped or grated onion
2 tablespoons chopped green pepper
1 teaspoon salt
1 egg
Drippings or other fat or oil
1 cup tomato juice or puree
1 tablespoon flour

Mix all ingredients except fat, tomato juice, and flour. Form into 4 or 5 flat cakes.

Brown the cakes on both sides in fat or oil in a fry pan. Add tomato juice, cover, and simmer slowly until done, about 25 minutes.

Remove cakes and keep them hot. Mix flour with a little water and stir slowly into the liquid in the pan. Cook until thickened, stirring occasionally. Serve this sauce with the cakes.

Menu Suggestion

Serve with mashed or buttered squash and apple-celery-raisin salad. Add protein to the meal with peanut butter cookies or cheese and crackers for dessert.

With Cooked Meat and Potatoes

Meat and Potato Cakes.—Combine 1½ cups diced or chopped cooked meat, 2 cups mashed potatoes, 1 egg, and 2 tablespoons chopped parsley. Mold into flat cakes, flour lightly, and brown in a little hot fat or oil.

Ham and scalloped potatoes

4 medium-sized potatoes, sliced

1 tablespoon grated onion
2 cups hot milk
½ pound thinly sliced ham, cut in serving pieces
Salt, pepper

Put half of the potatoes into a greased baking dish. Sprinkle with half the onion, a little salt, and pepper. Use salt sparingly.

Add ham. Cover with rest of potatoes, seasonings, and onion.

Add milk until it barely shows between the potato slices on top. Save rest of milk to add during cooking if needed.

Cover dish and bake at 350° F. (moderate oven) about 1 hour. Remove cover last 15 or 20 minutes to allow potatoes to brown on top.

Menu Suggestion

Serve with tomato juice, snap beans, and cabbage salad. Choose a fruit dessert such as dried-fruit whip.

Other Potato-Meat Dishes

Use ham trimmings, cheese, roast meat, chipped dried beef, frankfurters, or corned beef in place of ham in the recipe above.

Mashed Potato-Meat Pie.—Moisten leftover mashed potatoes with hot milk and beat until fluffy. Put a meat stew in a baking dish, top with the potatoes, and brown lightly at 400° F. (hot oven).

Liver loaf

1½ pounds liver
2 tablespoons fat or meat drippings
¼ cup chopped onion

    ¼ cup chopped celery
    ¼ pound pork sausage
    1 teaspoon salt
    1 cup soft breadcrumbs, mashed potatoes, or cooked rice
    1 egg, beaten
    About ⅔ cup milk or canned tomatoes

Brown the liver lightly in the fat. Chop fine.

Brown the onion and celery in the fat and add to the liver.

Add the rest of the ingredients, using just enough milk or tomatoes to moisten the mixture well.

Pack firmly into a loaf pan to shape. Bake in the pan or turn out on a rack in a shallow pan for baking. Bake at 350° F. (moderate oven) 1½ to 2 hours.

Menu Suggestion

Serve the loaf with spanish sauce (see recipe), buttered carrots, tossed green salad, and ice cream or fruit gelatin.

Spanish sauce

    2 tablespoons chopped onion
    2 tablespoons fat or meat drippings
    1 tablespoon flour
    2 cups cooked tomatoes
    ½ cup chopped celery
    ½ cup chopped green pepper
    Salt and pepper

Brown the onion in the fat and blend in the flour. Add the other ingredients and cook about 20 minutes, or until rather thick.

Tongue-and-corn casserole

    3 tablespoons butter or margarine
    1 teaspoon finely chopped onion
    2 tablespoons finely chopped pimiento
    3½ tablespoons flour
    1¼ cups milk, broth from tongue, or water with 2 beef bouillon cubes
    ¼ teaspoon salt
    1½ cups chopped cooked tongue
    1⅓ cups whole-grain corn, drained
    ⅓ cup grated cheese
    ¼ cup fine dry breadcrumbs mixed with butter or margarine

Melt butter or margarine and blend in flour and salt. Stir in the liquid, and cook and stir over low heat until thick and smooth.

Add rest of ingredients except breadcrumbs, and mix well.

Turn the mixture into a greased shallow baking dish and sprinkle top with crumbs.

Bake at 350° F. (moderate oven) 20 to 30 minutes, or until sauce is bubbly and crumbs are brown.

Menu Suggestion

Serve with raw cranberry relish and Swiss chard or kale, with pumpkin custard for dessert.

For Variety

In place of tongue use 1½ cups of chopped cooked meat such as chicken, turkey, or rabbit—or 4 frankfurters cut in thin crosswise slices. Brown the meat lightly in the butter or margarine before adding the flour, salt, and pepper.

Poultry ...

Like other meats, poultry has protein of high quality and is a good source of iron and the B vitamin niacin.

In retail markets poultry is usually sold "ready-to-cook"; occasionally, "dressed" or live. Ready-to-cook style comes either whole or cut up, and either freshly eviscerated or frozen; some is labeled to show government inspection and grading, some inspection only.

"Dressed" means that only blood and feathers have been removed. "Ready-to-cook" means that blood, feathers, head, feet, and viscera have been removed, and the bird has been thoroughly cleaned inside and out.

Price per pound of a dressed bird includes weight of head, feet, and viscera. A ready-to-cook bird is weighed and priced after this waste is removed. Therefore, though the price per pound is lower for the dressed bird, the cost per pound of actual poultry meat is about the same in the two styles.

Most chickens are sold in the following classes at these ages and weights:

Class	Age	Ready-to-cook weight
		Pounds
Broilers or fryers	8 to 10 weeks	1½ to 2½.
Roasters	3 to 5 months	2½ to 4½.
Stewing chickens	over 10 months	2 to 5½.

Stewing chickens—sometimes called "fowl" or "hens"—are hens old enough so that the tip of the breastbone has hardened. They need long slow cooking with steam or water to make the meat tender. They are often a good buy because they tend to have a higher proportion of meat to bone than younger chickens. A 5-pound dressed hen (3¾ pounds ready-to-cook) will give about 4 cups cooked meat coarsely cut, enough for at least two meals for a family of four if extended dishes are used—10 to 11 servings each containing 2 ounces of chicken.

Turkeys are sold in three classes based on weight and age: (1) Fryers or roasters, (2) young hens and young toms, (3) hens and toms. A fryer-roaster turkey, or a quarter or half of a larger turkey is often an economical roast, and can be made as attractive as the traditional big bird.

Stewed or steamed whole chicken

Prepare a fully drawn stewing chicken for cooking: Pull out pin-feathers and singe bird over flame; wash well, rinse, and dry. Clean giblets.

Stewed Whole Chicken.—Place the bird on a rack in a kettle and add water to half cover bird. Salt water lightly. Cover kettle and simmer until chicken is tender, turning occasionally for even cooking. Three to 4 hours will probably be needed.

Cook giblets with the chicken, removing them as soon as done.

Cool chicken in broth, breast down, an hour or more.

The cooked whole bird may be browned with or without stuffing. Coat it with fat, place it breast up on a rack in a shallow open pan, and brown at about 350° F. (moderate oven).

Steamed Whole Chicken.—Follow the same general directions as for stewing, but add water only to the level of the rack in the kettle and keep the bird breast up all the time. As the water boils away, add more. Steaming time will be 2 to 3 hours.

Stewed or Steamed Chicken, in Pieces

Cut a stewing chicken into pieces suitable for serving. Simmer in water to cover, or steam. Pieces take about as long to cook as a whole bird.

Chicken with dumplings

    1 stewing chicken cut in pieces and stewed
    3 to 4 cups broth
    6 tablespoons chicken fat
    3 to 6 tablespoons flour
    Salt and pepper

Remove pieces of chicken from the broth and keep them hot. Skim fat from broth.

Blend fat and flour, stir in several spoonfuls of the broth, and pour the mixture into the rest of the broth, stirring constantly.

Cook this gravy until it is slightly thickened. Season to taste.

Dumplings

    ¾ cup sifted flour
    2½ teaspoons baking powder
    ½ teaspoon salt
    1 egg
    ⅓ cup milk

Sift flour, baking powder, and salt together.

Beat egg, add milk, and mix with the dry ingredients.

Drop by small spoonfuls on boiling chicken gravy, cover tightly, and cook 15 minutes. The cover must not be removed while the dumplings are cooking, for if the steam escapes they will not be light.

Menu Suggestion

Serve with broccoli or other green vegetable, gelatin vegetable salad, date-and-nut pudding.

Curried chicken with carrots

    1 stewing chicken cut in pieces and stewed or steamed
    3 tablespoons chicken fat
    1 pint chicken broth
    ½ cup sliced onion
    3 tablespoons flour
    ¼ teaspoon curry powder
    2 cups cooked shredded carrots
    Salt

Take cooked chicken from the broth. Skim off fat and measure quantities of fat and broth needed.

Make sauce: Cook onion in fat for a few minutes. Blend in flour and curry powder. Add broth, and cook until smooth and thickened, stirring constantly.

Mix chicken and carrots with sauce. Add salt to taste.

Leftover cooked lamb, pork, or veal may be used instead of chicken.

Menu Suggestion

Serve with a border of flaky rice and a green vegetable. Start the meal with tomato juice and have fruit sundae for dessert.

For a company meal pass a relish dish of several of the following: Chopped hard-cooked eggs, chopped peanuts, sweet pickle relish, finely diced celery, chopped raw onion. Include shredded fresh coconut, too, if you live where it is available and inexpensive. Guests can sprinkle these tidbits over the rice and chicken as desired.

Roast turkey quarter or half

You can roast turkey quarters or halves stuffed or unstuffed.

Rub inside of cleaned turkey part with salt. To keep meat from drying, fasten skin with skewers over meat at bone edge all around cavity. Or with big needle and heavy cord, lace across cavity, catching the skin with each stitch.

On a front quarter or half, sew wing tightly to body or fasten with skewers put in firmly at an angle. On a rear quarter or half, sew drumstick to tail.

Stuffing may be baked separately while the turkey cooks or, if preferred, quarters or halves may be stuffed and then roasted. Use heavy paper to hold stuffing in place and lace cord across paper from side to side, catching skin with each stitch.

Place turkey part, skin side up, on a rack in roasting pan. Cover with thin greased cloth or brush skin with fat. Do not add water. Do not cover pan. Roast at 325° F. (slow oven), basting several times with drippings.

Quarters weighing 3½ to 5 pounds require 3 to 3½ hours to roast; those weighing 5 to 8 pounds, 3½ to 4 hours. A half turkey weighing 7 to 9 pounds ready-to-cook takes 3¾ to 4½ hours. A larger half-bird takes longer.

Serve with mashed potatoes or turnips, snap beans, cranberry relish, and fruit or fruit pie.

Cooked and canned meats and poultry ...

You can often save time and money by purchasing meat that will serve for two or more meals. Buy a smoked pork shoulder, a pot roast, or a stewing hen and plan your menus for several days around it.

Since meat is one of our more expensive foods, you may want to economize by reducing the size of meat servings. But meat is one of our best-liked foods. We want to keep the savory meat flavor in main dishes and provide enough protein in the family diet, too. Fortunately, both economy and sturdy meat servings can be achieved by wise use of meat-extending main dishes, using cooked and canned meats.

Least expensive of the meat extenders are the cereal foods—breadcrumbs in meat loaf, biscuit topping on a chicken pie, macaroni with meat in Italian-style dishes, rice cooked in chicken stock as in chicken risotto. The meat protein supplements the protein in the cereals and the result is a nutritious main dish.

Or you may want to extend a comparatively small amount of cooked meat with other high-protein foods such as milk, eggs, or cheese. These are the makings of such main dishes as creamed lamb, ham and egg scramble, or a beef and vegetable casserole with grated cheese on top.

When there is too little meat left for the basis of a main dish, use these small amounts for flavor and whatever protein they give. Try bits of cooked meats or poultry to season scalloped potatoes, macaroni, soups, salads, or sandwich spreads. Chop crusty brown chicken or turkey skin and add to gravy or a casserole mixture.

Some of the cooked luncheon meats are relatively low-priced and are as protein-rich as many of the more expensive meats. For example, a pound of bologna has as much protein as a pound of smoked ham and even a little more than a pound of beef with a moderate amount of bone and fat. Some of the canned meats provide economical main dishes, too, especially when extended with other foods.

Cool quickly any leftover meat, broth, or gravy (set pan in iced or very cold water); refrigerate at once. Store in the coldest part of the refrigerator. Cooked meat loses flavor quickly; cover or wrap loosely and plan to use within 1 or 2 days. Broth, gravy, and sauce made with meat are highly perishable. Store these covered and use within 1 or 2 days.

On the following pages are suggestions for extended dishes using cooked and canned meat and poultry. Other recipes will be found in the section on cereal foods.

Browned hash

1½ cups chopped cooked meat
3 cups chopped cooked potatoes
1 onion, finely chopped
Broth or milk
Seasoning to taste

The meat, potatoes, and onion may be chopped by hand or put through the food chopper, depending on the texture desired. Mix meat, potatoes, and onion thoroughly. Moisten with a little broth or milk, if desired, and season to taste. Spread mixture in an even layer in a lightly greased fry pan.

Cook slowly until browned on the bottom. If desired, turn and brown on the other side.

Turn hash out on a platter and garnish with parsley.

Menu Suggestion

Serve with cream of tomato soup, cooked green cabbage with grated cheese, and baked apple.

For Variety

Hash Cakes.—Make the meat and vegetable mixture into flat cakes and fry slowly on both sides until crusty.

Pork and Potato Fry.—Chop 1½ cups canned cured pork loaf and brown it lightly in a fry pan. Add 3 cups sliced or diced cooked potatoes and cook until brown on one side. Turn and brown on the other side.

Chop suey

    1 medium-sized onion, sliced thin
    1 green pepper, cut in slivers
    1½ tablespoons cooking fat or oil
    1½ cups celery, cut in slivers
    2 hard tart apples
    1 cup thin gravy or broth
    1½ cups cooked and diced lean pork
    Soy sauce and salt

Brown onion and green pepper in fat or oil.

Mix in the celery and the apple cut into small thin slices.

Add gravy or meat broth. Cover and cook 5 minutes.

Add meat and season to taste with soy sauce and salt. If desired, thicken with a little cornstarch mixed with water.

Heat thoroughly.

Menu Suggestion

Serve with flaky cooked rice, beets, lettuce salad, almond or oatmeal cookies.

For Variety

Cooked chicken, turkey, or beef may be used in the chop suey instead of pork.

Other vegetables may be used—carrots, radishes, Jerusalem artichokes, bean sprouts. Brazil nuts, thinly sliced, are also good.

Fried noodles may also be served with the chop suey mixture to add crispness.

Chicken a la king

   3 tablespoons chicken fat or butter or margarine
   2 tablespoons flour
   ½ cup milk
   1 cup chicken broth
   Salt and pepper
   ½ green pepper, diced
   ½ cup mushrooms, cut in pieces
   1 egg yolk
   1½ cups diced cooked chicken
   1 pimiento, chopped

Make white sauce: Melt 2 tablespoons of the fat and stir in the flour. Add milk and broth and cook until thickened, stirring constantly. Season with salt and pepper.

Melt the remaining tablespoon of fat, add green pepper and mushrooms and cook a few minutes over low heat.

Beat egg yolk, stir in a little of the sauce, and add to rest of sauce. Add the rest of the ingredients and cook until mixture is hot.

Serve in patty shells or on crisp toast, mashed potatoes, or waffles.

Menu Suggestion

Serve with green peas, carrot and raisin salad, and lemon chiffon pie.

For Variety

Cooked turkey, giblets, ham, veal, pork, or tuna fish may be used instead of chicken.

Cooked rabbit meat may be used. Add ½ teaspoon grated onion and ½ tablespoon lemon juice to the recipe for chicken a la king.

Chicken timbales

    1½ cups cooked rice
    1½ cups diced cooked chicken
    1 tablespoon finely diced onion
    2 eggs, beaten
    1 cup milk
    ⅓ cup chicken broth or milk
    ½ teaspoon salt
    Pepper

Mix all ingredients together. Divide mixture among custard cups or individual baking dishes.

Place cups in pan of very hot water and bake at 350° F. (moderate oven) about 30 minutes or until a knife inserted in the center of timbale comes out clean.

Menu Suggestion

Serve with glazed carrots, spinach with lemon, pear salad with cream or cottage cheese and nuts, and gingerbread for dessert.

For Variety

Cooked ham, pork, turkey, fish, or rabbit may be used in place of the chicken.

If you have less than the 1½ cups of chicken (or other meat) the recipe calls for, stretch the meat with sliced hard-cooked eggs and cooked peas. For a company meal, add mushrooms, fresh or canned.

Mushroom sauce may be served on the timbales.

Cooked macaroni, spaghetti, or noodles may be substituted for the cooked rice.

Luncheon-meat cups

    2 tablespoons butter or margarine
    2 tablespoons flour
    1 cup milk
    Salt and pepper
    2 cups cooked peas, seasoned
    1 tablespoon cooking oil or fat
    8 thin slices luncheon meat

Make white sauce: Melt the butter or margarine, blend in the flour, and add milk slowly. Cook until thickened, stirring constantly. Add salt and pepper to taste.

Add peas to sauce and heat.

Heat fat or oil and brown luncheon meat, allowing edges to curl to form cups. Put 2 cups together for each serving and fill with the hot creamed peas.

Menu Suggestion

Serve with hash browned potatoes and a mixed fruit salad, with baked custard or whipped gelatin dessert.

Other Ways to Use Luncheon Meat

Broiled.—Brush luncheon-meat slices with fat. Broil lightly. Serve with broiled tomato slices sprinkled with grated cheese.

"Birds."—Place stuffing on thin slices of luncheon meat, roll, and fasten with skewers or toothpicks. Brown lightly and cover the pan until the birds heat through.

Salad.—Mix diced luncheon meat with chopped pickles, celery, and carrots. Add salad dressing.

Curried lamb

    1 cup diced celery with tops
    1 small onion, diced
    3 tablespoons cooking fat or oil
    2 cups diced cooked lean lamb
    ¾ cup brown gravy
    Curry powder
    2 drops tabasco sauce
    Salt

Brown celery and onion slowly in the fat or oil.

Add meat, gravy, and seasonings. Use ⅛ to 1 teaspoon curry powder, as desired.

Stir over low heat until well mixed and hot. If too dry, add boiling water.

Menu Suggestion

Serve with flaky cooked rice, snap beans, coleslaw, and for dessert sweetpotato pie or pineapple chiffon pie.

For Variety

To make a savory meat pie: Omit the curry powder and tabasco sauce. Pour heated meat, vegetables, and gravy into a casserole and top with crisp, golden-brown baking-powder biscuits just before serving.

Green peas and small potatoes may be added to or used in place of the onions and celery in the meat pie.

Serve crisp tossed lettuce salad with the meat pie, and for dessert have a pineapple and orange fruit cup and oatmeal cookies made with raisins and peanuts.

Frankfurter and potato soup

   2 cups diced potatoes
   1 small onion, sliced
   1½ cups boiling water
   4 frankfurters
   1¾ teaspoons salt
   Pepper
   2 cups milk
   2 tablespoons finely chopped parsley

Cook potatoes and onion in boiling water until soft. Put through a ricer or mash slightly.

Cut frankfurters into ¼-inch slices.

Add frankfurters, seasonings, and milk to potato mixture.

Heat thoroughly, add parsley, and serve.

Menu Suggestion

Serve with a salad of chopped lettuce, tomato, and celery. Have dried-fruit upside-down cake for dessert. Cooked apricots and prunes make a colorful cake.

For Variety

Salami or other luncheon meat, cut in pieces, may be used instead of frankfurters. Allow one slice per person. Or sprinkle the soup with chopped cooked ham before serving.

Fresh sausage also may be used. Dice or crumble the meat and fry until crisp before adding it to the soup.

Pork souffle

2½ tablespoons butter or margarine
2½ tablespoons flour
1 cup milk
3 eggs, separated
1⅓ cups finely chopped cooked or canned pork
1 teaspoon finely chopped onion, or onion juice
2 teaspoons finely chopped green pepper
½ teaspoon salt

Make a thick white sauce: Melt the butter or margarine, blend in the flour, and add the milk. Stir and cook over low heat or hot water until thickened. Cook a little longer, and cool slightly.

Beat the egg yolks and blend into the cooled sauce. Stir in the meat, onion, and green pepper.

Add the salt to the egg whites and beat until stiff but not dry. Blend the meat mixture into the egg whites.

Turn into a shallow greased baking dish set in a pan of hot water.

Bake at 325° F. (slow oven) about 50 minutes, or until set and lightly browned. Serve at once.

Menu Suggestion

Serve with brussels sprouts or panned cabbage, lettuce salad, and hot apple cobbler for dessert.

For Variety

Stuffed Green Peppers.—Fill 4 parboiled peppers with chopped pork mixed with onion, salt, and enough gravy, broth, or cream to moisten. Set peppers in water in muffin cups and bake at 350° F. (moderate oven) 20 to 30 minutes.

Fish ...

Fish—fresh, frozen, canned, or salted—provides high-quality protein. And it lends interesting flavor and variety to meal planning.

Different kinds of fish vary greatly in price per pound. Some cost twice as much as others, depending on the season, local supply, and the preference of buyers.

Fresh fish may be whole, drawn, dressed, or in fillets or steaks. Whole fish are sold as they are caught. Drawn fish have only the viscera removed. Dressed fish have the viscera, head, tail, and usually the fins removed. Fillets are boneless slices of fish cut lengthwise away from the backbone. Steaks are crosswise slices, usually ¾ to 1 inch thick, still including bones.

There is no bone or waste in fish fillets, and very little in fish steaks—only about 9 percent. Dressed whole fish may be cheaper per pound but remember that they include considerable waste.

To provide the suggested 2 ounces of protein for 4 servings of a main dish, you will usually need to buy 2 pounds of whole fish. The exact amount needed depends on the kind of fish and the amount of waste in cleaning. It takes only 1 pound of boneless fillets or steaks to provide enough protein for 4 servings.

Some fish contain more fat than others. Fat fish are usually best for baking and broiling. And lean fish are better for cooking in water or steam or for making chowders, and for deep-fat or pan frying.

Frozen fish are a boon to inlanders. They give us the fish we want at any time of year. And the flavor is fresh. Before cooking a frozen fish, thaw it slowly if there is time—in a refrigerator or other cold place. If you are in a hurry, cook it slowly for a longer period. Never permit frozen fish to thaw and refreeze.

Canned fish is economical and convenient for family meals. It can be chilled and served in salads or on cold plate lunches with little further preparation. For cooked dishes, the brine or oil in which the fish is packed can often be used to add flavor and nutritive value to the sauce.

Salmon is ordinarily available in several different quality grades and is packed in brine. Mackerel also is packed in brine. Tuna fish may be had in solid-pack, chunk, or grated style, packed in oil or brine. Flaked fish—cod, haddock, pollack, or a combination—is ordinarily packed dry. Small domestic sardines packed in oil, mustard sauce, or tomato sauce are gaining market prominence.

Fish patties

1½ cups flaked cooked or canned fish
1½ cups dry mashed potatoes
1 tablespoon finely chopped onion
½ teaspoon salt
1 egg
Pepper
Flour
Cooking fat or oil

Combine all ingredients except flour and fat or oil.

Shape mixture into patties, roll in flour, and brown in fat or oil.

Menu Suggestion

Serve with pickled beets, a green vegetable, celery, and for dessert molded cornstarch pudding with a sauce of cooked dried apricots.

For Variety

Fish-Potato Puffs.—Add 2 egg yolks instead of a whole egg to the mixture of fish and potato; add seasonings and fold in stiffly beaten egg whites. Put mixture into greased custard cups and bake at 350° F. (moderate oven) 30 minutes.

Salt fish Balls.—Use 1 cup of salt fish. Soak the fish in lukewarm water until freshened, changing the water once or twice. An hour or two is usually long enough. Simmer in water until tender, drain, and shred. Stir fish into mashed potatoes. Omit onion and salt. Mix well with the other ingredients. Form into balls and roll in flour. Fry in shallow or deep fat, or bake in the oven.

Fish and noodles

    3 tablespoons chopped onion
    ⅓ cup diced celery
    1 tablespoon cooking fat or oil
    ½ teaspoon salt
    Pepper
    1⅔ cups cooked or canned tomatoes, or 2 cups raw tomatoes cut in pieces
    1⅔ cups cooked noodles
    2 cups flaked cooked fish
    Crumbs mixed with melted butter or margarine

Cook onion and celery in fat or oil a few minutes.

Add salt, pepper, and tomatoes and heat to boiling.

Put alternate layers of noodles, fish, and hot tomato mixture into a greased baking dish. Top with crumbs.

Bake at 350° F. (moderate oven) 20 minutes or until the mixture is heated through and the crumbs are browned.

Menu Suggestion

Serve with snap beans or asparagus, a green salad with a tangy horseradish dressing, and have cupcakes for dessert.

For Variety

Use cooked spaghetti or macaroni instead of noodles.

Instead of tomatoes, use cheese sauce—a thin white sauce to which ½ cup grated sharp cheese has been added for each cup of sauce. Sprinkle with grated cheese the last 10 minutes of baking.

Jellied tuna salad

    1 tablespoon unflavored gelatin
    ¼ cup cold water
    ½ teaspoon salt
    ½ teaspoon celery seed
    ¼ cup vinegar
    ¼ cup water
    2 eggs, beaten
    2 cups flaked canned tuna (or other canned or cooked fish)

Soften gelatin on top of water. Add seasonings, vinegar, and water to eggs. Cook over boiling water until thickened, stirring constantly.

Add gelatin and stir until it is dissolved.

Add fish and mix thoroughly. Pour into individual molds or large ring mold and chill.

Menu Suggestion

Serve scalloped potatoes with chives, cooked carrots, and have floating island with a topping of a bright, tart jelly for dessert.

For Variety

A Hearty Salad.—Place cold flaked cooked fish in lettuce cups. Surround with slices of tomatoes and cucumbers (in season), and very thin slices of cold boiled potato dipped in french dressing. Garnish with hard-cooked eggs.

A Cold Platter.—Serve chilled salmon which has been boned and cut into serving-size pieces. Surround with slices of tomatoes and mounds of tossed green salad.

Fried fish fillets

> 1 pound fish fillets (salmon, cod, rosefish, or haddock)
> Milk, flour
> 1 egg, beaten
> 1 tablespoon water
> ¾ tablespoon salt
> 1 cup fine dry crumbs
> Cooking fat or oil

Cut fish in serving pieces. Dip in milk, then in flour. Mix egg, water, and salt. Dip floured fish in this mixture, and roll in crumbs.

Heat fat or oil in fry pan, put in the fillets. Reduce heat, and cook slowly 10 to 15 minutes, until the fish is done through and golden brown on both sides. Drain.

Garnish with parsley and lemon.

Menu Suggestion

Serve with baked potatoes, creamed onions, asparagus salad or mixed vegetable salad, and gelatin fruit dessert.

For Variety

Oven-Fried Fillets.—Prepare fish for frying and place in greased shallow baking pan with space between pieces. Dot with butter or margarine, and bake at 500° F. (extremely hot oven) for 10 minutes.

Fish Baked in Milk.—Place fish in shallow baking pan, pour on ½ cup top milk. Sprinkle with salt, dot with butter or margarine. Bake at 350° F. (moderate oven) about 25 minutes.

Salmon loaf

    2 cups flaked canned or cooked salmon
    3 tablespoons cooking fat or oil
    3 tablespoons flour
    1 cup milk and salmon liquid
    Salt and pepper
    2 tablespoons finely chopped parsley
    2 cups soft bread cubes
    1 egg, beaten

Drain canned salmon, saving the liquid.

Make sauce: Heat fat or oil, blend in flour. Add enough milk to the salmon liquid to make 1 cup, and stir into the flour mixture. Cook until thickened, stirring constantly. Season.

Mix the sauce with the other ingredients. Form into loaf.

Bake in uncovered pan at 350° F. (moderate oven) about half an hour, or until brown.

Menu Suggestion

Serve with baked sweetpotatoes, creamed celery or peas, a green vegetable salad, and a fruit whip.

For Variety

To give extra flavor to salmon loaf, add ½ cup coarsely chopped sweet pickle and 1 teaspoon grated onion to mixture before baking.

Use cooked cod or haddock in place of the salmon.

Serve fish loaf with egg sauce made by adding to 1 cup white sauce, 2 sliced hard-cooked eggs and ½ to 1 tablespoon grated horseradish.

Stuffed fish fillets

¾ cup finely cut celery
3 tablespoons finely chopped onion
6 tablespoons cooking fat or oil
3 cups bread cubes
¾ teaspoon salt
Pepper
2 tablespoons chopped parsley
1 teaspoon thyme or other savory seasoning
1 pound small fish fillets
Fine dry crumbs
2 tablespoons fat

Cook celery and onion in fat or oil for a few minutes.

Add bread cubes and seasonings, and mix well.

Place stuffing on skin side of salted individual fillets. Roll and fasten with toothpicks.

Roll the stuffed fillets in fine crumbs and brown in fat in a fry pan. Cover and cook over low heat until tender—about 10 minutes.

Menu Suggestion

Serve with tartar sauce, boiled or baked potatoes or squash, green lima beans, cabbage and carrot salad, and lemon pie.

For Variety

Lay one fillet in greased baking dish; brush with melted fat or with oil, sprinkle with lemon juice, and cover with stuffing. Place second fillet on stuffing, sprinkle with crumbs, dot with fat, and bake uncovered at 350° F. (moderate oven) about 35 minutes. Baste occasionally with melted fat.

Fish with curry sauce

    1½ pounds dressed fish
    2 tablespoons butter or margarine
    1 tablespoon chopped green pepper
    1 small onion, chopped
    ¼ cup chopped celery
    2 tablespoons flour
    1 cup liquid (liquid from simmered fish plus milk)
    Curry powder
    Salt
    2 to 3 cups hot cooked rice
    2 tablespoons chopped parsley

Simmer fish about 10 minutes in a small quantity of water in a shallow pan. Drain and save liquid.

While the fish is cooking, make sauce: Melt the butter or margarine and cook the green pepper, onion, and celery in it a few minutes. Stir in the flour, then add the liquid. Cook until thickened, stirring constantly.

Add curry powder and salt to taste. Use ⅛ to 1 teaspoon curry powder, as desired.

Remove skin and bones from the cooked fish. Arrange fish on a hot platter with a border of flaky rice. Pour sauce over fish, and sprinkle parsley on top.

Menu Suggestion

Serve with a cooked green or yellow vegetable, citrus fruit salad, and cottage pudding with caramel sauce.

For Variety

Shrimp With Curry Sauce.—Instead of the fish, use shrimp.

Salmon, rice, and tomatoes

¼ cup chopped onion
¼ cup chopped green pepper
2 tablespoons bacon fat or meat drippings
1½ cups boiling water
2 cups cooked or canned tomatoes, or 2½ cups chopped raw tomatoes
Salt and pepper
⅓ cup raw rice
¼ cup chopped olives
2 cups flaked canned or cooked salmon

Cook onion and green pepper in the fat in a large fry pan until the onion is yellow. Add water, tomatoes, and salt and pepper to taste. Bring to boil.

Add rice and simmer until rice is tender—20 to 25 minutes—adding more water if needed.

Add olives and fish and cook 2 or 3 minutes longer to blend the flavors.

Menu Suggestion

Serve with baked squash, a green vegetable in salad or cooked, with cream pie for dessert.

For Variety

Other cooked fish may be used in place of salmon.

One cup of cooked rice may be used instead of the uncooked rice. Omit boiling water. Add the rice, olives, and fish as soon as the vegetables are tender and cook 5 or 10 minutes longer.

Celery may be used instead of the green pepper.

Eggs ...

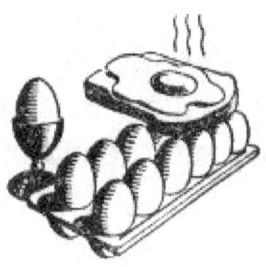

Eggs are excellent for main dishes because they contain high-quality protein, and are a good source of several important minerals and vitamins. When you serve eggs as an alternate for meat in a main dish, either allow more than 1 egg per person or add enough milk or cheese, as in cheese omelet, for example, to make up the difference.

Government-graded eggs are sold in cartons labeled with the grade (quality), size (weight), and date of grading. There are four U. S. grades—AA, A, B, and C. Grades AA and A have a large proportion of thick white, a firm high yolk, and a delicate flavor. They are often preferred for cooking in the shell, poaching, and frying. Grades B and C, which are less expensive than the two top grades, are a thrifty choice where appearance and delicate flavor are less important, as in Spanish omelet, gingerbread, or scrambled eggs with bacon.

Sizes of eggs and their minimum weights per dozen are:

Jumbo	30 ounces
Extra large	27 ounces
Large	24 ounces
Medium	21 ounces
Small	18 ounces
Peewee	15 ounces

Within any grade, large eggs usually cost more per dozen than smaller ones. Use the above weights to determine which size gives you the best return for your money. For instance, if medium eggs weighing 21 ounces are 56 cents a dozen (2⅔ cents an ounce) they are a better buy than large eggs weighing 24 ounces at 66 cents a dozen (2¾ cents an ounce).

Eggs are cheaper than meat as a source of main-dish protein when the price of eight large eggs is less than the price of a pound of meat with moderate amounts of bone and fat, such as rump roast. Or when the price of a dozen large eggs is less than the price of a pound of lean meat with little fat and bone, as round steak.

The color of the eggshell depends on the breed of hen and does not indicate the food value of the eggs. So do not pay a higher price for brown eggs than for white ones, or vice versa, with the idea that you are getting more food value.

Hot deviled eggs

    2 tablespoons butter, margarine, or oil
    ½ green pepper, chopped fine
    ⅓ cup celery, chopped fine
    1 small onion, chopped fine
    1 tablespoon flour
    1⅓ cups cooked or canned tomatoes
    1 teaspoon salt
    1 teaspoon worcestershire sauce
    2 drops tabasco sauce
    ⅔ cup cold milk
    6 hard-cooked eggs, sliced
    Crumbs, butter or margarine

Heat butter or margarine and cook chopped vegetables in it until they are tender. Blend in the flour.

Add tomatoes and seasonings and cook until thickened, stirring constantly.

Stir the hot tomato mixture into the milk and carefully add the eggs.

Turn into a greased baking dish and top with crumbs. Dot with butter or margarine and bake at 375° F. (moderate oven) until the crumbs are brown and the mixture is hot, about 10 to 15 minutes.

Menu Suggestion

Serve with asparagus, broccoli, or other green vegetable, mashed potatoes, and cheese with fruit pie for dessert.

For Variety

Instead of adding crumbs and baking the deviled egg mixture, serve it on toast or in patty shells.

Egg and toast special

    4 slices bacon, chopped fine
    4 thick slices bread, with 2-inch holes in centers
    4 eggs
    Salt and pepper

Cook bacon in a fry pan until half done; push to side of pan. Pour off fat. Brown bread slices in pan while bacon continues to cook.

Break the eggs into the holes, and season. Sprinkle bacon over eggs and bread. Reduce heat, cover pan, and cook until eggs are done.

Serve with creamed onions, sliced tomato and cottage cheese salad for needed protein, and a fruit dessert.

Mexican scrambled eggs

2 tablespoons minced onion
   ½ clove garlic, chopped fine
   1 small green pepper, diced fine
   2 tablespoons cooking fat or oil
   ⅓ cup sieved cooked or canned tomatoes
   3 tablespoons water
   1 teaspoon salt, pepper
   6 eggs, slightly beaten

Fry onion, garlic, and green pepper in fat or oil. Add tomatoes, water, salt, and pepper.

Cook 3 minutes. Add eggs and cook over low heat, stirring occasionally, until thickened.

Serve with potatoes, snap beans, green salad with strips of meat and cheese, and upside-down cake made with fresh or stewed dried fruit.

Shirred eggs on spinach

   1 to 1½ pounds spinach
   ½ teaspoon salt
   2 slices bacon
   Salt and pepper
   4 eggs

Wash spinach thoroughly, place in pan, and add salt. Cover and cook without added water until wilted—about 5 minutes.

Chop bacon fine; fry until crisp.

Mix bacon and bacon fat with spinach and season to taste with salt and pepper.

Place hot spinach in a baking dish. Make four depressions in spinach, and break an egg into each.

Cover dish and bake at 350° F. (moderate oven) 20 to 25 minutes or until eggs are firm. If desired, sprinkle grated cheese over the eggs during the last 10 minutes.

Menu Suggestion

Serve with baked sweetpotatoes, fruit salad, and cheese cake or pie with cheese.

For Variety

Shirred Eggs With Cheese.—Place a tablespoon of top milk in a greased custard cup. Break an egg into the cup, add salt and pepper, and bake at 350° F. (moderate oven) until white is nearly firm. Sprinkle with grated cheese and bake until cheese is melted.

Eggs scrambled with luncheon meat

    1 cup diced luncheon meat
    1 tablespoon cooking fat or oil
    4 eggs, beaten
    ¼ cup milk
    ¼ teaspoon salt
    Pepper

Salami, canned cured pork loaf, bologna, frankfurters, or any other spiced or smoked luncheon meat makes a good combination with eggs for this quick dinner dish.

Lightly brown the diced meat in the fat or oil in a fry pan over moderate heat.

Combine eggs, milk, salt, and pepper and add to the meat.

Cook, stirring constantly, until eggs are done.

Menu Suggestion

Serve with baked potatoes, carrot and celery sticks, and tomato aspic salad. Have fruit dumplings for dessert.

For Variety

Use *chopped cooked chicken, turkey, rabbit, or giblets*. With poultry, substitute broth for the milk for more flavor.

Or, instead of meat, use *¾ cup cottage cheese or chopped Cheddar cheese*, adding the cheese to the egg mixture before cooking. Serve these scrambled eggs with broiled, fried, or stewed tomatoes, or with tomato sauce.

Eggaroni

    4 hard-cooked eggs
    2 tablespoons butter or margarine
    2 tablespoons flour
    1⅔ cups milk
    1 teaspoon finely chopped onion
    ½ tablespoon horseradish, if desired
    1½ cups cooked macaroni
    Salt and pepper
    2 tomatoes, cut in quarters
    Crumbs mixed with melted butter or margarine

Cut eggs in quarters.

Make white sauce: Melt butter or margarine, blend in flour, and add milk slowly. Cook, stirring, until thickened.

Add other ingredients except tomatoes and crumbs. Pour into greased baking dish.

Press tomatoes into top of mixture, leaving skin surface exposed.

Sprinkle crumbs over top and bake at 350° F. (moderate oven) 20 to 30 minutes or until tomatoes are tender.

Menu Suggestion

Serve with spinach or kale, apple and raisin salad, and apricot snow with custard sauce.

For Variety

Cover macaroni mixture with pieces of canned, instead of fresh, tomatoes. Make sauce with juice from tomatoes instead of milk.

Omit tomatoes. Mix ½ cup grated cheese with the crumbs and sprinkle over top during last 15 minutes of baking.

Puffy spanish omelet

    1 cup cooked or canned tomatoes, or 1¼ cups chopped raw tomatoes
    1 small green pepper, chopped
    ½ small onion, chopped fine
    1 tablespoon chopped parsley
    ¼ cup chopped celery
    8 to 10 stuffed olives, sliced
    4 eggs, separated
    ½ teaspoon salt
    ⅛ teaspoon pepper
    1 tablespoon cooking fat or oil

Combine tomatoes, green pepper, onion, parsley, celery, and olives. Simmer 15 minutes or until liquid is reduced to a few tablespoonfuls.

Beat egg yolks well. Add salt to egg whites and beat until stiff but not dry.

Gradually fold the beaten egg yolks into the whites and then fold in the cooked vegetables. Add pepper.

Heat the fat or oil in a fry pan and pour in the egg mixture. Cook over low heat until lightly browned on the bottom. Cover and cook until set.

Or, when the omelet is lightly browned on the bottom, finish by baking 10 to 15 minutes at 350° F. (moderate oven).

Menu Suggestion

Serve with slices of broiled ham or fried sausages for more protein, and with baked potatoes, greens, and cooked dried fruit.

Egg and potato scramble

    2 slices bacon
    4 medium-sized potatoes, sliced thin
    1 teaspoon salt
    4 eggs, beaten
    ¼ cup milk
    Pepper

Fry bacon slices and remove from fry pan.

Fry potatoes in the fat until they are well browned, sprinkling with salt as browning starts.

Cover pan closely. Cook over low heat until potatoes are tender.

Combine eggs, milk, and pepper. Pour over potatoes in pan and cook slowly, stirring occasionally, until eggs are set.

Crumble bacon slices and add just before removing pan from heat. Serve at once.

Menu Suggestion

Serve with scalloped tomatoes or eggplant, spinach or kale, pear and cottage cheese salad, cookies.

For Variety

Bits of cooked ham, chipped beef, or any cooked meats may be used in place of the bacon in this recipe. Thin slices of sausages or chopped chicken livers are especially good. Fry the potatoes in bacon fat or other meat drippings when omitting the bacon.

Small cubes of cheese or flakes of smoked fish are other welcome additions with their own distinctive flavors.

Eggs in potato nests

1½ cups leftover mashed potatoes
5 eggs
Salt and pepper

Mix potatoes with one of the eggs. Shape mixture into four balls, place on greased baking sheet.

Press centers of balls to make cups. Break an egg into each cup, season with salt and pepper.

Bake at 325° F. (slow oven) 20 to 25 minutes or until eggs are as firm as desired.

Menu Suggestion

Serve with broccoli and cheese sauce, and crisp salad, and spicecake for dessert.

For Variety

Add ¼ cup grated cheese and 1 teaspoon grated onion or onion juice to the potato mixture.

Bake the potato cups and fill with a mixture such as creamed salmon and peas or creamed chicken and celery.

Mix ¾ cup chopped cooked ham with 2 cups mashed potatoes; season. Add the yolk of 1 egg and fold in the stiffly beaten egg white. Line a greased baking dish with this mixture; bake 30 minutes at 350° F. (moderate oven) until potatoes are slightly browned. Fill the potato "nest" with hot creamed ham and eggs: 1½ cups white sauce, 4 hard-cooked eggs sliced, ¼ cup chopped cooked ham.

Cheese and milk ...

Cheese is one of the most popular alternates for meat. Like meat and eggs, it contains high-quality protein and is an excellent supplement for the protein in bread and such other cereal foods as macaroni, noodles, and spaghetti.

Cheese is not equal in food value to the milk from which it is made. It contains one of the milk proteins but the other is separated out when cheese is made and is left in the whey.

American Cheddar, sometimes called American or "store" cheese, is the cheese most commonly used in cooking in this country. It is sold in natural and processed forms, and varies in flavor from mild to very sharp. Other cheeses are noted for their distinctive flavors and are chiefly used for garnishing, as the grated hard Parmesan, or for eating alone, as the sweet Swiss and Brick or the salty Bleu and Gouda.

You can count on half a pound of Cheddar cheese (2 cups chopped or grated) to give you enough protein for 4 servings of a main dish, or about the same amount of protein as a pound of meat with a moderate amount of bone and fat.

Because Cheddar cheese is a concentrated food, it is generally used in relatively small amounts—less than half a pound for 4 servings. Then other protein-rich foods are added to the meal or included in the cheese dish to increase the protein content, as milk and eggs added to the cheese for a souffle or an omelet.

Cottage cheese is less concentrated than Cheddar cheese, with only four-fifths as much protein per pound. In using cottage cheese as a meat alternate, use about a fourth more by weight than you would of Cheddar cheese. For instance, it would take 10 ounces of cottage cheese (compared with 8 ounces of Cheddar cheese) to alternate for a pound of beef with a moderate amount of fat and bone. Ten ounces of cottage cheese measure about 1¼ cups; a pound measures a little more than 2 cups.

We lean heavily on milk as a source of our day's protein. But it takes almost 7 cups of fluid milk, or about 2 cups of nonfat dry milk, to provide enough protein for 4 servings of a main dish. So, although we sometimes use a milk soup or chowder as the main dish, we are more likely to spread our milk consumption throughout the day—in beverages, custards, or milk puddings. In many recipes, we can increase the milk value by using fluid and dry milk together.

Cheese puff

    6 slices bread
    1½ cups ground or grated cheese
    2 eggs
    1½ cups milk
    ½ teaspoon salt
    Pepper, paprika, and mustard if desired

Fit 3 slices of bread into the bottom of a greased baking dish. Sprinkle with half the cheese and cover with the rest of the bread.

Beat eggs, add milk and seasonings, pour over bread and cheese, and cover with rest of cheese.

Set baking dish in a pan of hot water and bake at 350° F. (moderate oven) about 40 minutes or until custard is set and bread is puffy.

Serve with lima beans or peas, beets, green salad, fruit cobbler.

Cheese fondue

    1½ cups milk
    1½ cups soft breadcrumbs
    1 cup chopped or grated cheese
    1 tablespoon butter or margarine
    ½ teaspoon salt
    3 eggs, separated

Scald milk. Add crumbs, cheese, butter or margarine, and salt.

Beat egg yolks; add milk mixture. Beat egg whites until stiff but not dry; fold into mixture.

Pour into greased baking dish. Bake at 350° F. (moderate oven) 30 minutes or until set.

Serve at once with baked squash, a green vegetable, apple-celery salad with nuts, and cookies.

Baked macaroni and cheese

    4 ounces macaroni (1 cup elbow or 1-inch pieces)
    1 quart boiling water
    1 teaspoon salt
    1½ cups water or fluid milk
    ⅓ cup dry milk, whole or nonfat
    1 tablespoon flour
    ½ teaspoon salt
    1 tablespoon butter or margarine
    1 cup chopped or grated cheese
    Crumbs, butter or margarine

Cook the macaroni in the boiling water with the teaspoon of salt for the length of time indicated on the package. Drain.

Put the 1½ cups of water or fluid milk into top of double boiler. Add dry milk, flour, and half teaspoon salt. Beat until smooth.

Cook over boiling water, stirring constantly until thickened. Add butter or margarine and cheese. Stir until they are melted.

Put macaroni into a greased baking dish. Pour on the cheese sauce.

Top with crumbs, dot with butter or margarine. Bake at 375° F. (moderate oven) until crumbs are brown and mixture is hot.

Menu Suggestion

Serve with beet greens, grated raw carrot salad, and cooked dried apricots or fresh fruit cup with cookies for dessert.

For Variety

Add grated onion or chopped green pepper to the sauce.

Cheese rabbit (rarebit)

    3 tablespoons butter or margarine
    3 tablespoons flour
    1 tablespoon finely chopped onion
    ¼ teaspoon salt
    ¼ teaspoon powdered dry mustard
    Paprika, if desired
    1½ cups milk
    ⅓ pound cheese, ground or grated (1½ cups)
    1 egg, beaten

Melt butter or margarine and blend in flour, onion, and seasonings. Add milk slowly. Cook over low heat until thickened, stirring constantly.

Remove from heat and add cheese.

Pour a little of the sauce into the beaten egg, then pour all back into the sauce. Stir and cook 2 or 3 minutes longer, until cheese is melted.

Serve on toast or crackers.

Menu Suggestion

Serve with lima beans or peas and combination vegetable salad. Have melon or other fresh fruit for dessert.

For Variety

Tomato rabbit.—Use tomato juice or thin tomato soup instead of milk in the recipe for Cheese Rabbit.

To make plain or tomato rabbit a heartier dish, serve over quartered hard-cooked eggs on toast.

Cottage cheese-pickle-peanut sandwich

⅔ cup cottage cheese
⅓ cup peanut butter, coarse grind
⅓ cup diced dill or sweet pickles
8 slices bread
2 tablespoons milk
¼ teaspoon salt
1 egg, beaten
Cooking fat or oil

Combine cottage cheese, peanut butter, and chopped pickles.

Spread the mixture generously on 4 bread slices and cover with the other 4 slices.

Add milk and salt to the beaten egg and mix thoroughly.

Dip both sides of sandwiches quickly into the egg mixture. Do not soak the bread. Brown on both sides in hot fat over moderate heat.

Menu Suggestion

Serve with vegetable soup or a large vegetable salad, and fresh fruit.

Cottage Cheese Salads

Season cottage cheese with finely chopped chives and use for stuffing fresh tomatoes. Or, in winter, use to fill the center of a ring mold of tomato aspic jelly.

Moisten cottage cheese with top milk and season with salt and pepper. Heap in the center of cantaloupe rings and top with pitted sweet cherries.

Dry beans and peas ...

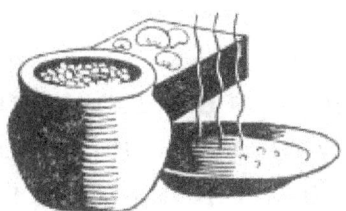

There are dozens of varieties of beans and peas, and for centuries they have been important in the diets of many peoples. In this country, varieties grown and used in some sections are practically unknown in others. The South has its blackeye peas and black beans, the East and Middle West have their pea beans, soybeans, and kidney beans, and the Southwest and West like pinto beans and chickpeas.

Beans and peas contain proteins that are not well balanced by themselves and need to be supplemented with high-quality protein in the same meal. When you serve beans as the main dish, you can increase the quality and quantity of protein in the meal by adding a little meat or cheese. This is done in many famous national bean dishes. For example, ham or smoked sausage is often added to split-pea soup and grated cheese is used to garnish beans.

When you serve beans alone as the main dish, you need to cook about 1⅓ cups, or a little more than 9 ounces of dry navy beans, to provide the amount of protein recommended for 4 servings. This makes about 3 cups of cooked beans, or four ¾-cup servings. If you do not use this amount or do not add other protein food to the bean dish, remember to supplement the protein elsewhere in the meal, perhaps with an egg salad or baked custard.

Soybean protein is of higher quality than protein of most beans commonly used in this country. For high nutritive value and distinctive flavor from your food dollar, use soybeans sometimes instead of navy or lima beans in favorite bean recipes, or use some soy flour in making breads and hot breads.

Split peas provide slightly more protein than an equal weight or measure of dry beans except soybeans. Try thick hot split-pea soup for the main dish on a cold winter day.

Beans and peas are economical protein foods. You will generally find that a protein dish made up partly of beans and providing an equal quantity of protein averages less in cost than one made up entirely of meat.

To soak dry beans and whole peas, boil them 2 minutes in the soaking water first, to help prevent fermentation and hardening of skins. An hour of soaking is enough after boiling, but overnight may be more convenient. Cook beans in the soaking water for best flavor and highest nutritive value. Split peas do not need soaking.

Baked chili beans and hamburger

1 cup dry chili or kidney beans
3 cups water
½ pound ground beef
2 tablespoons drippings or other fat
1 small onion, sliced
1 clove garlic, sliced
½ green pepper, chopped fine
2 cups cooked or canned tomatoes, or 2½ cups raw tomatoes cut in pieces
½ teaspoon salt
Chili powder to taste

Boil beans in water 2 minutes. Remove from heat, cover, and soak 1 hour or overnight. Cook in same water until almost tender.

Brown meat in fat. Add onion, garlic, green pepper, tomatoes, and salt, and cook a few minutes.

Add meat mixture and chili powder to beans.

Place in a baking dish or bean pot, cover, and bake at 350° F. (moderate oven) about 2 hours. Uncover during the last half hour to brown the beans if desired.

Or cook the mixture slowly for about 1 hour in a covered kettle on top of the range. Stir occasionally.

Menu Suggestion

Serve with a large garden salad and fruit betty or apple dumplings.

For Variety

Cook the beans with a ham bone, omitting ground beef and chili powder. Or use 1 cup ham trimmings from a baked ham instead of beef.

Dry bean or pea soup

    1 cup dry beans or whole peas
    6 cups water
    Meaty ham bone
    1 small onion, chopped
    Salt and pepper

Boil beans or peas in water 2 minutes. Remove from heat, cover, and soak 1 hour or overnight.

Add ham bone. Boil gently 2 hours in a covered pan.

Add onion and continue cooking 30 minutes, or until beans are soft. Remove bone and cut off meat.

Add meat to soup. Season to taste, and reheat.

Menu Suggestion

Serve with tomato aspic, or fruit salad, with cottage cheese. Have custard pie for dessert.

For Variety

For Thick, Smooth Soup.—Put beans or peas through a sieve before adding meat; discard skins. Mix 2 teaspoons flour with a little water; stir into soup. Boil 1 minute, stirring constantly.

Split-Pea or Lentil Soup.—Use 1 cup of split peas or lentils instead of beans in the recipe above. No soaking is needed. Boil gently, stirring occasionally, about 3 hours. Proceed as for bean soup.

Hot Pot.—Add a garlic clove and 2 chili peppers or a teaspoon of chili powder to beans before cooking. After cooking, remove garlic and peppers.

Quick baked beans

2 slices bacon
3 tablespoons finely chopped onion
1 tablespoon molasses
1½ tablespoons catsup
¼ teaspoon salt
¼ teaspoon powdered dry mustard
½ teaspoon worcestershire sauce, if desired
2 to 3 cups canned or cooked dry beans

Fry bacon, remove from pan, and cook onion for a few minutes in bacon fat.

Add molasses, catsup, salt, mustard, and worcestershire sauce.

Add beans and mix lightly. Pour into a baking dish. Crumble bacon and sprinkle over the top.

Bake 20 minutes at 350°F. (moderate oven). Or heat in a fry pan on top of range, and serve with bacon crumbled over the top.

Menu Suggestion

Serve with hot cornbread, carrot and cabbage slaw, with baked custard for dessert.

For Variety

Hot Bean Salad.—Omit molasses, add ¼ cup vinegar and ¼ cup water, and cook until the liquid is absorbed. To complete the meal serve quick-cooked green cabbage, crisp strips of celery and carrots, and pumpkin pie with cheese.

Creole Beans.—To 2 cups cooked beans add ½ teaspoon salt, ¼ cup each chopped green pepper and onion, and 1 cup canned tomatoes. Bake at 350° F. (moderate oven) 1 hour.

Soybean chop suey

    1 green pepper, shredded
    1½ cups shredded onion
    1½ tablespoons cooking fat or oil
    ¾ cup diced celery
    1½ cups cooked dry soybeans
    1½ cups meat broth
    ½ teaspoon salt
    2 teaspoons cornstarch
    2 tablespoons water
    1 cup quartered radishes or sliced carrots
    Soy sauce

Cook green pepper and onion in the fat or oil in a fry pan 3 or 4 minutes, turning them often.

Add celery, soybeans, broth, and salt. (Canned bouillon or bouillon cubes and water may be used in place of broth.)

Cover and simmer 5 to 8 minutes.

Blend cornstarch with water, stir into the mixture, and cook until thickened. Add radishes or carrots and soy sauce to taste.

Menu Suggestion

Serve with hot flaky rice, pineapple and cottage cheese salad, with ice cream for dessert.

Another Soybean Recipe

Soybean Souffle.—To 2 cups cooked dry soybeans, ground or sieved, add 2 beaten egg yolks. Season with chopped onion, parsley, salt, and pepper. Fold in stiffly beaten whites of eggs. Pour into a greased baking dish and bake at 350°F. (moderate oven) about 30 minutes or until set.

Bean chowder

    1 cup dry beans
    1 quart water
    ¾ cup chopped carrots
    ¾ cup cooked or canned tomatoes, or 1 cup chopped raw tomatoes
    1 onion, finely chopped
    ⅓ cup shredded green pepper
    1 tablespoon flour
    1½ cups milk
    Salt and pepper

Boil beans in water for 2 minutes. Remove from heat, cover, and soak 1 hour or overnight.

Cook beans in covered pan until they begin to soften. Add vegetables; cook until tender.

Mix flour with a little water and stir into vegetables. Cook 10 minutes longer, stirring occasionally to prevent sticking.

Add milk and seasonings, heat to boiling, and serve.

Menu Suggestion

Serve with a peanut-and-fruit salad—sections of grapefruit and orange—and for dessert, prune whip with custard sauce.

For Variety

Baked Bean Chowder.—Use leftover baked beans. Cook ¾ cup diced carrots, ⅓ cup green pepper, and 1 onion in 1½ cups water, until tender. Add ¾ cup canned tomatoes, 2 cups baked beans, and seasonings, and reheat. Blend 1 tablespoon flour and 2 tablespoons cold water and stir into the vegetables. Cook 10 minutes. Add 1½ cups of milk; reheat.

Savory bean stew

    1 cup dry beans or whole peas
    1 quart water
    ¼ cup diced salt pork
    ⅓ cup chopped onion
    ½ pound chopped beef
    2 to 2½ cups cooked or canned tomatoes, or 2½ to 3 cups chopped raw tomatoes
    Salt and pepper

Boil beans or peas in the water 2 minutes. Remove from heat, cover, and soak 1 hour or overnight.

Fry salt pork until crisp, remove from pan, and brown onion in the fat. Add meat and stir and cook slowly a few minutes.

Combine all ingredients, season, and simmer until meat is tender and flavors are blended.

Menu Suggestion

Serve with squash, a shredded raw vegetable salad, and lemon sponge pudding.

For Variety

Chili Con Carne.—Add 2 to 4 teaspoons chili powder and a little garlic to recipe. Red kidney, and the pink beans of the West, are favorites for this dish.

Hopping John.—Add ½ cup dry blackeye peas to 2¼ cups ham broth. Boil 2 minutes, soak 1 hour or overnight. Cook covered until almost tender. Add ½ cup raw rice, ½ cup chopped cooked ham. Cook gently 20 to 30 minutes. The broth should be almost gone when the rice is tender.

Bread and other cereal foods ...

Bread and other cereal foods are truly the staff of life for some families and are used for all or part of the main dish for many of their meals. Griddlecakes, toast, or oatmeal is a favorite breakfast dish. And sandwiches, spaghetti, or macaroni may form the bulk of a noon or evening meal.

Bread and other cereal foods do not provide large amounts of protein in any one serving. But, because we eat bread and other cereals so often, grain foods contribute a fourth of the protein in diets in this country. The cereal foods also contribute to our diets more calories, more iron, and more thiamine than any other group of foods.

Grains cannot make an adequate main dish unless eaten in large quantities or combined with protein-rich foods.

A few figures on grain proteins may be helpful. A pound loaf of whole-wheat bread contains a little less than three-fourths as much protein as a pound of beef with a moderate amount of fat and bone. You would need to eat one-third of the loaf, seven or eight slices, for as much protein as you get in a fourth pound of the meat—an average serving.

A pound loaf of white bread contains somewhat less protein than a pound whole-wheat loaf. The use of nonfat dry milk solids in bread increases quantity and quality of proteins slightly.

Proteins from bread and other cereal foods are not of as high quality as proteins of animal products, although some are better than others. You can somewhat increase the protein values obtained from cereals by using whole-wheat bread and whole-grain breakfast cereals and by adding corn germ or wheat germ to other cereals. Milk, eggs, soy flour or grits, meat, or fish help to bring up the protein content and protein value of a cereal main dish.

Familiar examples of the cereal-extended main dishes are creamed chicken or fish—or meat in brown sauce—served with toast, noodles, spaghetti, rice, or hominy grits. Other popular combinations of cereals with high-protein foods are scrapple, macaroni or rice with cheese, eggs with toast, and meat loaf or patties with breadcrumbs. And we are also extending high-protein foods with cereals when we add biscuit to the meat stew, dumplings to stewed chicken, and waffles to the breakfast or supper sausages.

Oatmeal griddlecakes with sausages

2 cups milk
2 cups quick-cooking oats
⅓ cup sifted flour
2½ teaspoons baking powder
1 teaspoon salt
2 eggs, separated
⅓ cup cooking fat or oil
Cooked sausages

Heat milk and pour it over the oats. Allow to cool.

Sift together flour, baking powder, and salt.

Beat egg yolks and add to oat mixture. Add melted fat or oil and stir in dry ingredients.

Fold in stiffly beaten egg whites.

Drop the batter by spoonfuls on a hot greased griddle. When the surface is covered with bubbles, turn and brown on the other side. Oatmeal griddlecakes take longer to brown than plain griddlecakes.

Menu Suggestion

Serve the griddlecakes with sirup and the sausages. The rest of the meal may be a large fruit and carrot salad and gingerbread.

For Variety

Apple Griddlecakes.—Add ¼ teaspoon cinnamon, 2 tablespoons brown sugar, and 1 cup finely chopped, pared apples to the batter before adding egg whites.

French toast with tomato-meat sauce

 2 eggs
 ⅓ cup milk
 ¼ teaspoon salt
 8 slices bread
 Cooking fat or oil

Beat eggs, add milk and salt. Dip bread quickly into mixture. Brown on both sides in a little fat or oil, using moderate heat.

Tomato-meat sauce

 2 cups canned tomatoes or 2½ cups chopped raw tomatoes
 ½ pound chopped raw beef
 2 tablespoons chopped onion
 2 tablespoons chopped green pepper
 Cooking fat or oil

    1 tablespoon flour
    Salt and pepper

If using raw tomatoes cook them until soft. Press tomatoes through a sieve.

Brown beef, onion, and green pepper in the fat or oil. Blend in the flour, add tomatoes slowly. Season. Cook and stir over low heat until as thick as desired.

Menu Suggestion

Serve with a green vegetable, peanut and cabbage salad, and fruit and cheese for dessert.

For Variety

Serve the toast with cheese sauce and omit dessert cheese.

Whole-wheat scrapple

    2 pounds fresh pork (bony cut)
    1½ quarts water
    1½ cups uncooked fine whole-wheat cereal
    1 small onion, chopped fine
    Salt and pepper

Cook pork slowly in the water until the meat drops from the bones. Strain off the broth.

Separate bones from meat, taking care to get out all the tiny pieces. Cut meat fine.

Add water to the broth, if necessary, to make 1 quart. Bring to boil and slowly stir in the cereal. Cook until the mixture is thickened, stirring constantly.

Add meat and onion. Cook 15 minutes longer, stirring frequently. Season with salt and pepper.

Pour the mixture into loaf pans and let stand until cool and firm.

To serve, slice scrapple and brown slowly on both sides in a hot fry pan. If the scrapple is rich with fat, extra fat is not needed for browning.

Menu Suggestion

Serve with baked sweetpotatoes, scalloped or fried apples or applesauce, a green salad, and lemon meringue pie.

For Variety

One cup *cornmeal* may be used instead of 1½ cups whole-wheat cereal.

Rice with chicken

    1½ cups diced leftover cooked chicken
    Chicken bones
    Salt
    1 onion, chopped fine
    1½ tablespoons chicken fat
    ½ cup raw rice
    Grated cheese

This dish may be made with more or less than 1½ cups chicken, but this amount is needed to give enough protein for a main dish for four persons.

Cover bones with water and simmer an hour or longer. Drain off the broth. Add any leftover chicken gravy and water, if needed, to make 1 quart broth. Add salt to taste.

In a large fry pan, cook onion a few minutes in chicken fat, add broth. When it boils up rapidly, add the rice slowly.

Cover the pan. Simmer rice about 25 minutes or until the grains swell and become soft. Stir with a fork from time to time to keep the rice from sticking.

By the time the rice is done, it will have absorbed the broth, and the grains will be large and separate. Then add the pieces of chicken and more salt if needed. Turn mixture onto a hot platter, and sprinkle generously with grated cheese.

Menu Suggestion

Serve with spinach and hard-cooked egg, celery and carrot sticks, fruit pickle, and apple or peach dumpling or pie.

Noodles, western style

    3 ounces noodles (about 1¼ cups broken noodles)
    ½ small green pepper, diced
    1½ tablespoons bacon fat or meat drippings
    1½ tablespoons flour
    2 cups cooked or canned tomatoes, or 2½ cups raw tomatoes cut in pieces
    1 tablespoon finely chopped parsley
    1 cup chipped corned beef, spiced ham, or dried beef
    ¼ teaspoon salt
    Pepper

Cook noodles 10 minutes in boiling salted water. Drain.

Cook green pepper in fat in large fry pan until tender.

Blend in flour and add other ingredients. Simmer 5 minutes to thicken. Add salt and pepper.

Add noodles and simmer 10 minutes longer.

Menu Suggestion

Serve with cooked cabbage sprinkled with cheese, and cooked carrots. Add a salad of apple, celery, and raisins, and have jellyroll for dessert.

Noodles in Another Way

Noodle Omelet.—Drain the cooked noodles; fry in a little fat or oil until golden brown. Add to 4 eggs, lightly beaten and seasoned with salt and pepper. Turn back into fry pan, and cook slowly until brown on bottom and set on top. Fold onto a hot platter.

Tamale pie

    1 cup cornmeal
    3 cups boiling water
    1½ teaspoons salt
    1 onion, chopped
    1 green pepper, chopped
    3 tablespoons cooking fat or oil
    ¾ pound chopped raw meat, or 1½ cups chopped cooked meat
    1½ cups drained canned or cooked tomatoes
    Chili powder and salt to taste

Stir cornmeal slowly into rapidly boiling salted water. Bring to boil over direct heat. Cover, and cook 45 minutes over boiling water, stirring occasionally.

Cook onion and green pepper in fat or oil until tender; remove. Add meat to fat. If raw meat is used, cook until done.

Add remaining ingredients and heat thoroughly.

Pour a layer of the cooked cornmeal into a greased baking dish, add meat mixture, and cover with the rest of the cornmeal.

Bake at 400° F. (hot oven) 30 minutes.

Menu Suggestion

Serve with crisp green salad with cheese dressing, and cherry tart.

Other Meat Pies

Leftover meat, gravy, and cooked vegetables may be used in meat pies. Heat together, put into a baking dish, and cover with rounds of baking-powder biscuit dough. Bake at 450° F. (very hot oven).

Lunch-box main dishes ...

Packing a really good lunch-box meal—one that is high in important food values and in appetite appeal—takes more careful planning than many a meal that goes on the family table. For lunch-box foods are necessarily limited to those that can be held for several hours without spoiling or losing their freshness. But there are foods that pack well, and ways to vary them, so packed lunches need not be monotonous.

Sandwiches tend to be the "backbone" of the lunch-box meal. And when the fillings are high in protein foods—meats, eggs, cheese, fish, peanut butter, baked beans—they really are main dishes. To increase the protein value of these sandwiches, be generous with the filling. One-fourth cup of filling, spread clear to the edge of the bread, or 2 slices of meat or cheese, is not too much. Salmon or egg salad on a roll is a better main dish and more appetizing if part of the roll is scooped out to make room for more filling. Use centers as bread crumbs.

Provide variety in sandwiches by using different kinds of bread. For instance, "cheese on rye" is a favorite, but cheese on raisin bread or Boston brown bread may be a welcome change.

Vary the fillings—spread salad dressing or prepared mustard, topped with sliced cucumber or a lettuce leaf, over the meat or cheese; spread a thin layer of jelly over the peanut butter. Try different kinds of cheese. Or make a cheese spread: Put cheese through the food chopper and add jam or mashed cooked fruit, or salad dressing with chopped onion or sweet pickle.

For food value and variety, pack a salad of raw fruits or vegetables with the sandwich lunch. If the sandwiches are a little low in protein, include cottage cheese in the salad. Even with dressing and greens, salad travels well in a covered container of paper, glass, or plastic.

Hot soups, stews, or chowders—made with meats, fish, or beans—are good winter additions to the sandwich lunch. An individual-size insulated bottle or wide-mouth container for them may be a good investment, if these hot dishes cannot be bought at school or at work.

Moist, soft sandwich filling or salad mixtures made with finely chopped meat, eggs, or fish with salad dressing spoil quickly when temperatures are high. Refrigerate all such mixtures immediately after buying or making them and use them within 2 days. Lunches containing these mixtures are best refrigerated if they have to stand more than 3 or 4 hours before they are eaten.

Salads

Ham and Egg.—For each serving, use 1 chopped hard-cooked egg, ¼ cup chopped cooked ham. Add onion, celery, green pepper, pickle, and salad dressing to taste.

Meat and Macaroni.—Mix equal parts of cooked meat and macaroni. Add chopped pickles and celery and moisten with salad dressing.

Meat and Bean.—Use shredded chipped beef, or chopped cooked corned beef. Mix with any kind of cooked dry beans; add diced onion and tart dressing.

Potato With Meat.—Mix cut-up ham or crumbled bacon with potatoes. Add cut-up pickles, celery, onion, and salad dressing.

Meat and Fruit.—Mix any cut-up cooked meat with celery and raisins or raw dried apricots. Add salt and salad dressing as needed.

Egg and Beet.—Combine sliced hard-cooked eggs and pickled beets. Add shredded endive or other salad greens. Pack dressing separately.

Kidney Bean.—Combine drained cooked kidney beans, cut-up celery, dill pickles, and cubed cheese. Add mayonnaise.

Fish.—Shred leftover cooked fish—halibut, salmon, or sardines. Combine with cut-up celery, cooked peas, lemon juice, and salad dressing.

Chicken.—Mix equal parts of cut-up cooked chicken and crisp celery. Add salad dressing and thin slices of sweet pickle or stuffed olives.

Sandwich fillings

Sliced Meat or Cheese.—Use two slices with vegetables between. Good combinations are: Beef with parsley or thinly sliced tomato and salad dressing; tongue with watercress and salad dressing or prepared mustard; cheese with either of the above combinations, or with jam, jelly, or marmalade.

Bacon.—Crumble crisp fried bacon, and add it to one of the following: Cottage cheese, sliced tomato, diced hard-cooked egg, raw carrots, onion, sweet or dill pickles.

Baked Bean.—Mash cold baked beans and moisten with thick chili sauce. Add diced sweet pickle and thinly sliced onion or cucumber.

Peanut Butter.—Mix equal parts of peanut butter and chopped raisins or other raw dried fruit. Or, mix the peanut butter with diced pickle and chopped onion.

Cheese Salad.—Dice cheese fine. Add a little chopped onion and green pepper or parsley, season, and moisten with salad dressing.

Cottage Cheese.—Mix cottage cheese with cut-up celery, a little grated carrot, diced pickles, and nuts.

Fish.—Mix flaked cooked fish with chopped cabbage, salad dressing, and salt to taste. Or mash sardines with hard-cooked egg.

Egg.—Combine diced hard-cooked egg, celery, and pickles with prepared mustard and salad dressing.

Other main dishes for the lunch box

Hot Soup.—Add thin slices of frankfurter or Vienna sausage to split-pea or bean soup. Pack some cheese to go with vegetable or cream soup or corn chowder. Heat soups very hot; pack in insulated container.

Meat Stews.—A favorite stew with vegetables and gravy, kept hot in an insulated container until lunch time, is a welcome winter dish.

Baked Beans, Corned Beef Hash, Creamed Meats, or Eggs.—These are cold-weather dishes. Pack hot in special insulated container.

Cheese.—A large slice of cheese or serving of cottage cheese teams well with fruit in summer lunches.

Deviled Eggs.—Mash, season, and moisten hard-cooked egg yolks as usual. Add finely chopped peanuts or cooked meat before stuffing the egg whites with the yolk mixture.

Chicken or Chop.—Yesterday's drumstick or pork chop makes a main dish to eat out of hand.

Sliced Meat.—Spread two slices of ham or other meat with chopped vegetables and salad dressing. Roll, and fasten with toothpicks.

Smoked Fish.—Bone and skin pieces; pack by themselves. Drain oil-packed sardines; wrap well.

Luncheon Meats.—Many ready-to-serve meats—liver sausage, bologna, salami, spiced meat loaves—give as high protein value per pound as fresh meats. Keep cold, add to lunch last.

To complete the lunch-box meal

Plan the lunch-box meal to include contrasts in flavors and textures. It is more appetizing when it contains something moist to offset the dry foods, tart foods to offset the sweet, and crisp foods as well as soft.

Relishes.—Raw vegetables and pickles add crispness to the sandwich lunch. Try carrot and celery sticks, pieces of cauliflower or turnip, sliced cucumber or onion, or crisp lettuce leaves rolled together.

Desserts.—With soup or salad, use cake or cookies for contrast. If the main dish is sandwiches, choose a juicy fresh fruit.

Fresh fruits are easy to pack and popular. As a change from the often-used apples, oranges, and bananas, try plums, grapes, and pears in season.

Baked and canned fruits travel well in covered containers—glass, plastic, or paper. Try an occasional baked pear or peach, as well as apple.

Sweet fruit desserts like pie or fruitcake or fruit-filled cookies taste best after a tart salad or a milk-flavored soup.

Baked custards are good to use when the main dish is low in protein. It is best not to use cake with cream filling, or cream pie or cream puffs. The fillings spoil easily in hot weather, or even in winter if the lunch is not kept in a cool place.